WESTERN BUTTERFLIES

for

Young Explorers

AN
A to Z
GUIDE

SHARON LAMAR

2014

MOUNTAIN PRESS PUBLISHING COMPANY

MISSOULA, MONTANA

I dedicate this book to all young explorers and those who are young at heart, especially Steve, Annie, and Lucas. —SL

Other books in this series

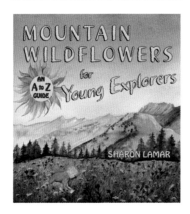

Library of Congress Cataloging-in-Publication Data

Lamar, Sharon, 1953-.
 Western butterflies for young explorers : an A to Z guide / Sharon Lamar.
     pages cm
 ISBN 978-0-87842-614-0 (pbk. : alk. paper)
 1. Butterflies—West (U.S.)—Identification—Juvenile literature. 2. Butterflies—West (U.S.)—
Pictorial works—Juvenile literature. I. Title.
 QL551.W3L36 2014
 595.78'90978--dc23
                        2013043708

Printed in Hong Kong by Mantec Production Company

Mountain Press
PUBLISHING COMPANY
P.O. Box 2399 · Missoula, MT 59806 · 406-728-1900
800-234-5308 · info@mtnpress.com
www.mountain-press.com

PREFACE

I'm not sure which butterfly sighting was most exciting as my husband and I hiked along Rose Creek amid the wildflowers in Glacier National Park on a warm spring day. We spotted Tiger Swallowtails in a thicket of alder shrubs, an Orangetip butterfly flashing its brilliant color, several Green Comma butterflies puddling near the creek, a Milbert's Tortoiseshell basking in the sun, many bright blue Spring Azures fluttering by, and numerous Mourning Cloaks soaring overhead—all along a two-mile stretch of trail!

Butterflies are one of earth's most magical creatures. What other animal transforms from a slow-moving, leaf-chewing, wormlike creature into a high-flying, multicolored, winged beauty? It's nature's most dramatic costume change! And you can watch it happen in your own backyard. Butterflies can be found just about anywhere, from vacant lots to woodlands, gardens, and even classrooms.

Raising Painted Lady butterflies was a favorite science activity of my students when I taught first grade. They learned about the life cycle of butterflies by observing the day-to-day change from egg to larva to pupa to adult. They were amazed when they witnessed a butterfly emerging from its chrysalis. Later on, they recognized a Painted Lady as we hiked near the Swan River. More than once I've been asked, "Do you think that's the same Painted Lady we released last week?"

This guide book is meant to be an introduction to the fascinating world of butterflies. Of the hundreds of butterflies in the western United States, I've chosen twenty-six of the most beautiful, common, or interesting butterflies, one for each letter of the alphabet. Each entry describes the butterfly, the caterpillar, the wingspan, habitat, range, and other interesting facts. I also made an effort to paint a true, life-size likeness of the butterflies.

As you pore over the images in this book, imagine the lives of the butterflies and the story they tell. Enjoy them on these pages, and then head outdoors to discover them for yourself!

BUTTERFLY LIFE CYCLE

The life of a butterfly begins with an egg. Most butterflies lay their eggs on the leaf or stem of the plant that the caterpillars eat, but some lay their eggs on the flower of the plant. The butterfly egg hatches into a caterpillar, or larva. It eats almost nonstop. Soon it outgrows its skin, sheds it, and grows a new skin. This process of growing and shedding skin is called molting. Each time it sheds its skin, it begins a new growth stage, known as an instar. Caterpillars usually pass through four or five instars. When the caterpillar is fully grown, it attaches itself to a twig or leaf. The body revealed by the last shedding of skin is called a pupa. It hardens into a protective covering called a chrysalis. In the pupa stage the caterpillar looks like a doll wrapped in a blanket. The complete change from a caterpillar to an adult butterfly, a process called metamorphosis, happens when it is a pupa. In the last stage of its life cycle, the adult butterfly emerges, starting the life cycle over once again.

Most flying insects die when winter comes, so how does the life cycle continue? Many butterfly species overwinter as eggs, larvae, or pupae before emerging in the spring. Imagine spending the winter wrapped up in a sleeping bag like a caterpillar in a chrysalis! Some butterflies overwinter as adults. They fatten up in the fall, just like bears, then find a tree hole, rock crevice, or brush pile in which to hibernate. Hibernating larvae, pupae, and butterflies increase the amount of sugar in their bodies to prevent them from freezing. A few amazing butterfly species even fly south in the fall to spend the winter in warmer climates!

BUTTERFLY BODY PARTS

Like other insects, butterflies have antennae, compound eyes, six legs, and a body that is divided into three parts: the head, the thorax, and the abdomen. Unlike other insects, however, a butterfly has wings covered by scales. The clubbed **antennae** are the primary sense organs that respond to smells, sounds, and vibrations. The **thorax** contains the muscles that control the wings and legs, while the **abdomen** holds the organs. The **proboscis**, located under the head, is used to suck nectar from flowers. The tips of the butterfly's feet have sensory organs that help it taste.

Butterflies have four wings, two in front (forewings) and two in back (hindwings). The tops, or uppersides, of the wings often look different from the bottoms, or undersides. Sometimes it is hard to distinguish the forewing from the hindwing when the wings are folded together. Many butterflies have wings with circular markings, called eyespots.

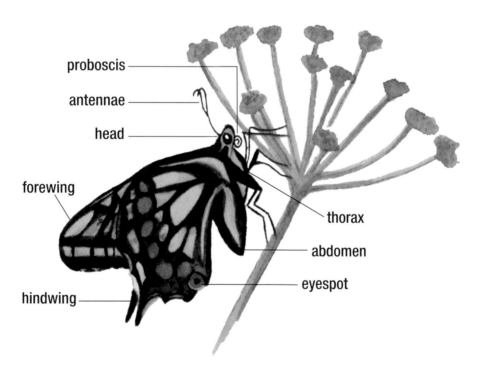

This butterfly is shown with wings folded.

BUTTERFLY CLASSIFICATION

Butterflies are insects, one of the most numerous animal groups on earth. Scientists combine butterflies and moths into the category of insects called Lepidoptera, which means "scaled wings." Their wings are covered with tiny overlapping scales. The easiest way to distinguish a butterfly from a moth is to look for a swelling at the tip of the antennae, which you will see on butterflies but not on moths. Each antenna looks like a miniature club. You can also tell moths and butterflies apart by the time of day you see them: butterflies are active mostly during the day whereas most moths are active at night.

Butterflies are divided into the following six families:

SWALLOWTAILS are the largest butterflies. Most have tails on their hindwings like the tail feathers on swallows, birds that zoom through the air catching insects. Swallowtails have a sailing or fluttering flight.

WHITES AND SULPHURS are mostly medium sized and white or yellow. They often fly low to the ground with a fluttering flight. Whites may sit with their wings open, but sulphurs sit with wings folded. Many whites and sulphurs visit drying mud puddles, where they feed on minerals from the soil.

GOSSAMER-WINGS have delicate, small features. Some larvae have honeydew glands that attract ants, which lick the honeydew off the caterpillars. In turn, the ants help protect the caterpillars and pupae from predators.

METALMARKS are found mainly in the American tropics. They are named for the gold, silver, and copper-colored scales on their wings. They usually land on the undersides of leaves, with their wings spread wide open.

BRUSHFOOT butterflies have a strong and rapid flight. They are called brushfoots because the front two legs have little brushes of hairs on them. The front legs are much smaller than the other four legs. Some species in this family are the longest-lived butterflies known, living over ten months as adults.

SKIPPERS get their name from their quick, darting flight. They seem to skip through the air. Skippers differ from the other five butterfly families in a few traits, including large eyes, short antennae (often with hooked clubs), and stout bodies.

ICONS

The small pictures below, called icons, appear on each butterfly page. They show you where to find specific types of information.

Wingspan: The distance from the tip of one pair of wings to the tip of the other pair.

Habitat: The place or environment where the butterfly spends its life.

Caterpillar: A description of the larva, or caterpillar.

Range: The area in western North America in which the butterfly is known to live.

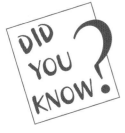

Did You Know: A fun fact about butterfly natural history. It may include information about such topics as migration, eating habits, flight speed, camouflage, and behavior.

Anise Swallowtail

Papilio zelicaon

SWALLOWTAIL FAMILY

The Anise Swallowtail is more yellow than black, with a yellow band running across the middle of the wings. Yellow spots also line the outside margins of both wings. The hindwings have blue spots between the yellow band and the medium-long tail. On the hindwings, the eyespot is orange with a black center. The abdomen is black with yellow side stripes.

The Anise Swallowtail lives throughout the West, from British Columbia south to Baja California and east to the eastern edge of the Rocky Mountains and in the Black Hills in South Dakota.

The larva is green with black bands and orange to yellow dots. It feeds on plants in the parsley family, including sweet fennel, which is also called anise.

Swallowtails are named for the tails on their hindwings that look like the long tail feathers of the birds called swallows. The tails help protect the Anise Swallowtail from predators. When the butterfly is at rest, with its wings folded, the tails look like antennae, while the spots on the hindwings look like eyes. This may fool its enemies into aiming for its tails, allowing the butterfly to escape.

WINGSPAN

2¾ to 3½ inches

Found in open spaces from sea level to 14,000-foot mountaintops.

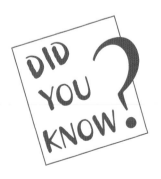

PLANT PICTURED
Sweet Fennel (Anise)

Buckeye (Common)

Junonia coenia
BRUSHFOOT FAMILY

The tops of the tannish brown wings have bold, colorful eyespots—one on each forewing, and two on each hindwing. Two orange bars are located on the upper edge of each forewing. The undersides of the forewings look like the uppersides in a lighter shade, while the hindwing undersides are dull brown with crescent-shaped markings.

The Common Buckeye lives in the southern United States and along the Pacific Coast. It migrates north to Oregon, Nevada, Idaho, and Wyoming.

The larva is dark, with a pale stripe on its back and white or orange side markings. It has black bristles on its back and red markings on its head. It feeds on plantains, monkeyflowers, and snapdragons.

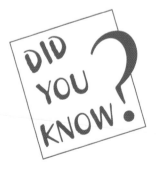
DID YOU KNOW?

Birds, lizards, mice, and spiders love to snack on butterflies, but butterflies have some tricks that can confuse these predators. The eyespots on the wings of the Common Buckeye help scare its enemies away. Predators think the spots are the eyes of a much larger animal, not the markings of a small insect.

WINGSPAN

1 ⅜ to 2 ½ inches

Prefers open, sunny areas in fields, marshes, meadows, swamps, and shorelines.

PLANT PICTURED
Marigolds

Cabbage White

Pieris rapae

<small>WHITE AND SULPHUR FAMILY</small>

The top surfaces of the hindwings and forewings are white, with a black patch on the tips of the forewings. The males have one black dot on each forewing, while females have two.

The Cabbage White is found throughout southern Canada and the continental United States, except in the extreme south.

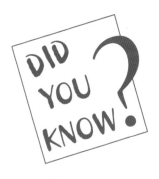

The bright green larva has many fine hairs and faint yellow side stripes. It feeds on plants in the mustard family, including cabbage, broccoli, and watercress.

Gardeners consider the Cabbage White caterpillar a pest because it feeds on cabbage, broccoli, cauliflower, and other members of the mustard family. Gardeners can protect their plants without harming the Cabbage White caterpillar. Rick Mikula, author of *The Family Butterfly Book*, suggests using a homemade remedy that repels caterpillars. Simply soak one cup of tomato leaves in two cups of water overnight, strain, and spray onto the plants.

WINGSPAN

1 ¾ to 2 ¼ inches

Prefers open areas, fields, gardens, and roadsides.

OTHER NAMES
Small White

PLANT PICTURED
Butte Marigolds

Desert Marble
Euchloe lotta
WHITE AND SULPHUR FAMILY

The tops of the wings are white, with a black bar close to the upper edge of each forewing. The undersides of the wings have grayish green marbling with pearly white areas in between the marbling.

1 ¼ to 1 ¾ inches

The Desert Marble ranges from southeast British Columbia south through the mountainous regions of the West.

Prefers deserts, rocky canyons, hills, ridges, and open pinyon-juniper woodlands.

The larva varies from green to grayish green, usually with a white stripe along each side and a purple band above. It feeds on plants in the mustard family, often tansy mustards and rock cresses.

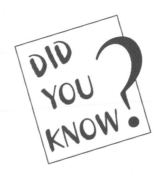

DID YOU KNOW?

Marble refers to the pattern on the underside of the Desert Marble's wings, which looks like marble rock or stone. This camouflage helps them blend into their surroundings and makes it nearly impossible to spot them. Many butterflies protect themselves from predators by having wings that look like dead leaves, the bark of trees, or rocks.

PLANT PICTURED
Scarlet Bee Balm

14

E

1 ⅜ to 1 ⅝ inches

Prefers grasslands, sagebrush, meadows, alpine trundra, and open woodlands.

PLANT PICTURED
Nasturtium

Edith's Checkerspot
Euphydryas editha
BRUSHFOOT FAMILY

The top surfaces of the wings look like a checkerboard with a pattern of orangish red, black, and cream. The forewings are rounded. The abdomen is black with reddish orange rings.

Edith's Checkerspot ranges from southern British Columbia and Alberta south through the Rocky Mountains to Baja California and southwestern Colorado.

The mature larva is black, speckled with white or orange markings, and has many black bristles. It feeds on Indian paintbrush, lousewort, and other plants.

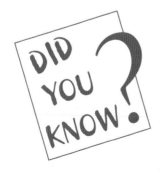

DID YOU KNOW?

Two subspecies of Edith's Checkerspot are listed under the Endangered Species Act—the Bay Checkerspot in the San Francisco Bay area and the Quino Checkerspot in southern California. The greatest threats to these butterflies are habitat loss and climate change.

F

WINGSPAN

1 ¼ to 1 ½ inches

Prefers meadows, fields, and streamsides from sea level to treeline in the mountains.

PLANT PICTURED
Cosmos

Field Crescent
Phyciodes pulchella
BRUSHFOOT FAMILY

The top sides of the wings are blackish brown with orange patches or spots. The forewings are rounded, and the tips of the antennae are brown. The undersides of the forewings are yellowish brown with black patches on the inner margin, while the undersides of the hindwings are yellowish brown with rusty markings.

The Field Crescent lives from central Alaska and northern Canada south to southern California, central Arizona, and southern New Mexico.

The larva is brown to black with faint stripes and tufts of spines. It feeds on plants in the aster family.

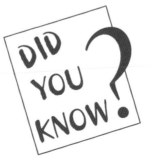

The Field Crescent is the most common crescent in the western United States. The young caterpillars often feed together. When half-grown, the caterpillars hibernate, emerging in spring to feed some more.

G

WINGSPAN

1 ¾ to 2 ½ inches

Prefers woodlands,
streamsides,
and canyons.

OTHER NAMES
Faunus Anglewing

PLANT PICTURED
Fireweed

Green Comma

Polygonia faunus
BRUSHFOOT FAMILY

The uppersides of the wings are burnt orange with brown patches and wide dark borders. The hindwing border has yellow spots. The edges of the wings look jagged. The undersides of the wings are grayish brown with a silver, comma-shaped spot in the center of the hindwing. The undersides often have mossy green spots along the margins.

The Green Comma is found from Alaska south through much of the mountainous west to central California and Colorado.

The larva is reddish or yellowish brown with a white patch and an orange band. The spines are white to brown. It feeds on willows, birches, and other plants.

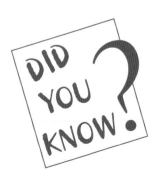

Green Comma butterflies survive the winter by crawling under the bark of trees, shingles, or the siding of houses and hibernating. They often emerge in early spring before any flowers have bloomed. This is not a problem for the Green Comma because it rarely feeds on flower nectar, instead preferring to feed on tree sap, which is plentiful in early spring. It also feeds on animal scat and carrion.

H

Hedgerow Hairstreak
Satyrium saepium
GOSSAMER-WING FAMILY

The uppersides of the wings are burnt orange with a thin black border. The tail is very short, tipped with white. The undersides are dull brown with a grayish blue spot near the tail.

WINGSPAN

1 to 1 ¼ inches

The Hedgerow Hairstreak inhabits the Pacific Coast from southern British Columbia south to Baja California and also lives in the Rocky Mountains from Montana south to northern Arizona and New Mexico.

The larva is light green with faint yellow stripes on its back and sides. It feeds on the ceanothus plant.

Prefers brushy areas and forests in the foothills and mountains.

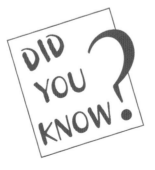
DID YOU KNOW?

The Hedgerow Hairstreak caterpillar emits a sugary solution, called honeydew, that attracts ants. They feed on it and protect the caterpillar by chasing off other predators and parasites, just like a bodyguard!

PLANT PICTURED
Iris

WINGSPAN

2 ½ to 3 inches

Prefers mountains, mountain deserts, and canyonlands.

OTHER NAMES
Short-tailed Black Swallowtail

PLANT PICTURED
Black-eyed Susan (Rudbeckia)

Indra Swallowtail

Papilio indra
SWALLOWTAIL FAMILY

The hindwings and forewings are mostly black with a thin pale yellow or cream band. The hindwing has several blue patches and an eyespot with a black center. The abdomen is mostly black. The tails can be very short to medium length.

The Indra Swallowtail occurs in all western states, except Texas and North Dakota.

The larva is usually black with pink, white, orange, or yellow marks. It feeds on plants in the parsley family.

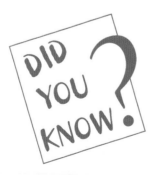

When threatened, caterpillars of the Swallowtail family defend themselves with a Y-shaped gland hidden under the skin behind the head. The gland produces a strong-smelling scent to repel enemies. When a predator comes near, the caterpillar can push out the gland to surprise or scare its enemies.

Jutta Arctic

Oeneis jutta

BRUSHFOOT FAMILY

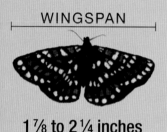

WINGSPAN

1 ⅞ to 2 ¼ inches

The uppersides of the wings are grayish brown with a band of yellowish orange spots. Most of the spots have black centers. The undersides of the wings look like bark. Usually, there are two eyespots on the forewing and one on the hindwing, and they have white centers. The edges are checkered brown and white.

The Jutta Arctic is found in alpine and subarctic habitats from Alaska, east across Canada to Maine, and south in the Rocky Mountains to Colorado.

Prefers lodgepole pine forests, wet tundra, and spruce bogs.

The larva is pale green with light stripes and reddish hairs. It feeds on sedges, including cottongrass.

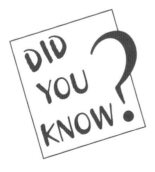

DID YOU KNOW?

In alpine and subarctic habitats, where the growing season is short, the Jutta Arctic larvae may live for two growing seasons (more than a year). After hatching from the egg, larvae begin to develop the first year, then overwinter and complete the life cycle the next year.

PLANT PICTURED
Wild Rose

K

Kricogonia lyside

Lyside Sulphur

WHITE AND SULPHUR FAMILY

The uppersides of the wings are pale yellow with a black bar on the edge of the hindwing. Males have a darker yellow patch on the undersides of the forewings. The color of the undersides of the wings varies from greenish yellow to pale yellow to almost white. The veins are visible on the undersides.

WINGSPAN

1 ½ to 2 ⅜ inches

The Lyside Sulphur is found from southern Texas and Arizona south to Venezuela. It sometimes strays as far north as Kansas, Nebraska, and Colorado.

Prefers lowland scrub and dry forest edges.

The larva is dull green with gray, brown, and yellow lines. It feeds on the Guayacan plant.

OTHER NAMES
Guayacan Sulphur

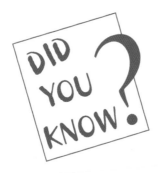

Butterflies fly best when the air temperature is 75 to 90 degrees Fahrenheit. Because butterflies are cold-blooded, they must bask in the sun's heat to warm up. Many butterflies open their wings to absorb the sun's warmth. Others, like the Lyside Sulphur, bask with their wings folded and facing the sun.

PLANT PICTURED
Pansy

28

L

Lorquin's Admiral

Limenitis lorquini
BRUSHFOOT FAMILY

The uppersides of the brownish black forewings are tipped with orange. A row of creamy white patches runs across the center of both wings like a big toothy grin. The undersides have gray, orangish brown, and white bands.

WINGSPAN

2 to 2⅝ inches

Prefers forest edges, mountain canyons, and streamsides.

The Lorquin's Admiral ranges from central British Columbia south to western Montana, Idaho, northwestern Nevada, and the Pacific Coast states.

The larva is grayish to olive brown with lighter patches and bumps on the body and a pair of spines behind the head. It usually feeds on willows.

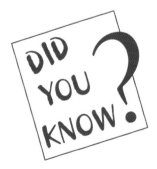

DID YOU KNOW?

The half-grown Lorquin's Admiral caterpillar spends the winter hibernating in a rolled leaf, called a hibernaculum. The caterpillar ties the leaf to the stem with a loop of silk so it doesn't fall off in winter. In addition to flower nectar, adult butterflies feed on bird droppings and dung!

PLANT PICTURED
Apple blossom

M

WINGSPAN

3 ½ to 4 inches

Found wherever milkweed grows, including prairies, foothills, fields, and roadsides.

PLANT PICTURED
Milkweed

Monarch

Danaus plexippus

BRUSHFOOT FAMILY

The uppersides of the wings are a bright, burnt orange with black veins and a black border. The wing margins have tiny white dots, which also occur on the body and abdomen. The male has a small black spot along the vein of the hindwing. The undersides of the wings are a paler orange.

Monarchs are found in southern Canada and all of the continental United States, except Alaska.

The larva, which has rings of white, yellow, and black, feeds on milkweed plants. The chemicals from the plant are absorbed in the caterpillar as it grows, making it distasteful to predators.

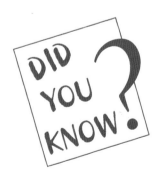

DID YOU KNOW?

Monarchs are long-distance flyers. In the autumn, they fly south to California and Mexico, migrating the way birds do. Swarms of them sleep together at night, often stopping at the same places year after year. In the spring the adults mate and begin to move north, laying eggs along the way. Their offspring then continue migrating northward, also pausing to breed and lay eggs. By summer, the next brood can be found across North America.

Northern Crescent

Phyciodes cocyta

BRUSHFOOT FAMILY

The uppersides of the wings are orange with black markings and margins. The undersides of the hindwings have a pale tan crescent patch and orange wormlike markings. The tips of the antennae are usually orange.

The Northern Crescent ranges from the Yukon south in the mountains of the West to northeastern Oregon, northeastern Nevada, central Arizona, and northern New Mexico.

Prefers woodland openings and edges, meadows, and streamsides.

The body of the larva is pinkish, and the spines are pinkish gray. The caterpillar feeds on asters.

PLANT PICTURED
Spotted Knapweed

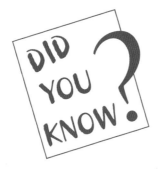

DID YOU KNOW?

Male Northern Crescent butterflies fly above the host plants looking for females to mate with, a behavior known as patrolling. Using its sense of smell and sight, the male is able to identify a female. The male sees the patterns on the female's wings with its compound eyes.

Orange Sulphur
Colias eurytheme
WHITE AND SULPHUR FAMILY

The uppersides of the wings are golden orange with a black border and a single black spot on the forewings. Underneath, the hindwings have one to two silver spots with smaller dark dots near the border. Both wings have a pink fringe.

The Orange Sulphur occurs from central Canada south throughout the continental United States.

The larva is dark green with a white stripe underlined with black on both sides. It feeds on legumes, especially alfalfa, white clover, and vetches.

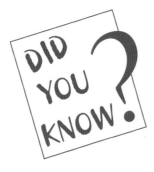

Male butterflies often visit mud puddles to feed on minerals from the soil. This behavior is known as puddling. Sulphur butterflies sometimes gather in large groups when puddling. When an enemy comes close, they rise up in a cloud. So many butterflies flying around confuses the predator, which may not catch anything.

WINGSPAN

1 ⅜ to 2 ¾ inches

Prefers open fields, especially clover and alfalfa fields, meadows, gardens, and prairies.

OTHER NAMES
Alfalfa Sulphur

PLANT PICTURED
Red Clover

Painted Lady

Vanessa cardui

BRUSHFOOT FAMILY

The uppersides of the wings look like a painting of orange, black, and white swirls of color. The hindwings have a row of five small black dots. The undersides are gray, brown, and black. The antennae are tipped with white.

Painted Ladies range throughout the continental United States and Canada. They can be found on all continents except Antarctica and Australia.

The larva has a black head and a greenish yellow body with black spots and spines on its back. It feeds on thistles as well as other plants.

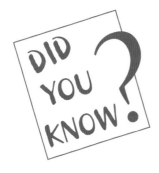

Like the Monarch butterfly, Painted Ladies migrate. Each spring they fly north, and in the fall, subsequent generations migrate to wintering areas in the south. Using radar to track their migration southward, scientists recently discovered that Painted Ladies fly at altitudes of up to 3,000 feet!

Queen Alexandra's Sulphur

Colias alexandra

WHITE AND SULPHUR FAMILY

The uppersides of the wings are lemon yellow with a thin black border. A small black spot is located on the forewings. The undersides of the hindwings are usually greenish yellow with a white spot in the center.

WINGSPAN

1 ¾ to 2 inches

Queen Alexandra's Sulphur ranges from British Columbia and Alberta south to Nevada and New Mexico.

Prefers open spaces, including prairies, grasslands, meadows, and forest openings.

The larva is green with white and yellowish orange stripes along its sides. It feeds on legume plants, including vetches and lupines.

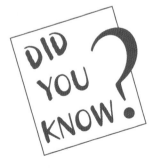

DID YOU KNOW?

Lepidopterist W. H. Edwards named this butterfly in 1863, the year the future Edward VII of England married Alexandra of Denmark, who became a very popular queen.

PLANT PICTURED
Canada Thistle

Red Admiral
Vanessa atalanta
BRUSHFOOT FAMILY

The uppersides are a rich dark brown with reddish orange stripes across the forewings, like the stripes navy admirals wear on their uniforms. Reddish orange stripes also edge the hindwings, forming a semicircle pattern with the forewing stripes. The tips of the forewings have white spots. The undersides of the forewings have bands of red, white, and blue, while the hindwing undersides look like bark.

The Red Admiral can be found anywhere in the continental United States.

A fully grown larva is patterned with light and dark markings from black and yellow to brown and tan. It feeds on plants in the nettle family.

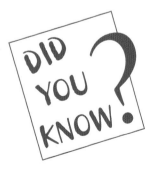

Female Red Admiral butterflies lay their eggs on nettles, often considered a weed. English statesman Winston Churchill allowed stinging nettles to grow in his garden because he wanted to attract Red Admiral butterflies. In addition to flower nectar, adult Red Admirals feed on juice from rotting fruit, tree sap, and bird droppings.

WINGSPAN

1 ¾ to 3 inches

Prefers forests, canyons, meadows, streamsides, and gardens.

OTHER NAMES
Alderman Butterfly

PLANT PICTURED
Leafy Aster

S

1 ⅜ to 1 ⅞ inches

Prefers open forests, streamsides, roads, and rocky canyons.

PLANT PICTURED
Blue Violet

Stella Orangetip
Anthocharis stella
White and Sulphur Family

The uppersides of the male's forewings are creamy white, while the female's forewings are pale yellow. The tip of the forewing is reddish orange with a black border. The undersides of the hindwings have olive green to gray marbling.

The Stella Orangetip occurs from southern British Columbia and southwestern Alberta south to northern Utah and Wyoming.

The larva is dull green with a large head. The body is covered with short black hairs. The larva feeds on plants in the mustard family.

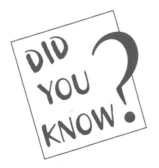

DID YOU KNOW?

The Stella Orangetip hibernates in the pupa stage. As with all butterflies, the hibernating form—the larva, pupa, or adult butterfly—increases the amount of sugar in its body to prevent it from freezing—a natural antifreeze!

Tiger Swallowtail (Western)

Papilio rutulus

SWALLOWTAIL FAMILY

The uppersides and undersides of the wings have black and yellow stripes like a tiger. The hindwings have one to two orange spots and several blue spots near the tail.

WINGSPAN

2 ¾ to 3 ⅞ inches

Western Tiger Swallowtails range from British Columbia south to Baja California and east to the Rocky Mountains and Black Hills.

Prefers open areas in mountain woodlands and canyons, often near streams.

The larva is green with a red Y-shaped horn behind its head. It has two orange eyespots with a dark center and a yellow back band. It feeds on the leaves of cottonwood, ash, willow, alder, aspen, and other plants.

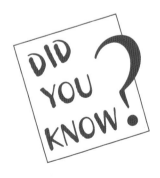

DID YOU KNOW?

The Tiger Swallowtail caterpillar protects itself from predators in several ways. The early-stage larvae look like bird droppings, an unusual disguise! After molting two or three times, the caterpillar turns green with large yellow eyespots. The eyespots make the larva look like a fierce snake. It also has a hornlike gland that releases a strong smell to scare away enemies.

PLANT PICTURED
Wilson's Penstemon

Uncas Skipper

Hesperia uncas

SKIPPER FAMILY

The Uncas Skipper has short antennae, large eyes, and a stout body. The uppersides of the wings are brownish orange but darker along the edges. The undersides of the rounded hindwings have white veins with white spots along the veins.

The Uncas Skipper can be found in the high plains from central Alberta east to southern Manitoba and south to central California, southeast Arizona, and northwest Texas.

The head of the larva is dark brown with cream-colored marks, while the body is tan. This caterpillar feeds on grasses like blue grama and needlegrass.

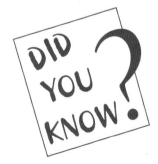

Skippers are some of the fastest butterflies. Some skippers can fly 30 miles per hour or faster, while slow-flying butterflies fly at 5 miles per hour.

WINGSPAN

1 ⅛ to 1 ⅝ inches

Prefers short-grass prairies, sagebrush, and open woodlands.

OTHER NAMES
White-vein Skipper

PLANT PICTURED
Lance-leaf Coreopsis

V

2 ½ to 3 ⅜ inches

Prefers meadows, fields, marshes, streamsides, and forest edges.

PLANT PICTURED
Zinnia

Viceroy
Limenitis archippus
BRUSHFOOT FAMILY

The wings are burnt orange with black veins, both above and below, but the undersides are paler. The edges of the wings have a row of white spots. To distinguish the Viceroy from the Monarch butterfly, look for the black line that curves across the hindwings of the Viceroy.

The Viceroy is found in most of the continental United States and southern Canada.

The larva looks like a bird dropping, olive brown with a white saddle patch. It has bumps on its body and two bristles behind its head. It feeds on the leaves of willows, poplars, and cottonwoods.

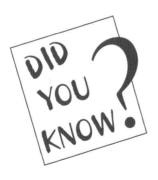

DID YOU KNOW?

The Viceroy is a copycat! The pattern and color of the Viceroy butterfly's wings are nearly the same as the Monarch butterfly's pattern, except for a black line across its hindwings. These two equally toxic butterfly species mimic each other to the benefit of each. Predators avoid them because they are distasteful. In addition to flower nectar, adult Viceroy butterflies feed on aphid honeydew, dung, and carrion.

Western Tailed Blue

Cupido amyntula

GOSSAMER-WING FAMILY

The uppersides of the male's wings are purplish blue, while the female's uppersides are brown with some blue at the lower margin. The undersides are powdery gray with black spots. There is a narrow tail on the hindwing.

WINGSPAN

⅞ to 1 ⅛ inches

Prefers open areas with low shrubs, including forest meadows and streamsides.

PLANT PICTURED
Blanketflower

The Western Tailed Blue is found in all western mountainous regions from northern Alaska to northern Baja California.

The larva varies in color from green to yellow green and may have pink or maroon marks. It feeds on legume plants, especially vetches.

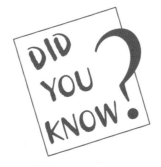

The Western Tailed Blue caterpillar eats the seeds of a legume pod, seals the pod with silk, then spends the winter inside the pod.

Xami Hairstreak

Callophrys xami

GOSSAMER-WING FAMILY

The uppersides of the wings are golden brown. The hindwings have one short and one long tail. The undersides of the hindwings are yellowish green with a white line forming a W near the tails.

¾ to 1 ¼ inches

In the United States, the Xami Hairstreak can be found in central Texas, southwest New Mexico, and southeast Arizona.

Prefers dry, rocky canyons and slopes.

The larva is yellowish green with reddish marks. It feeds on sedum, along with other plants.

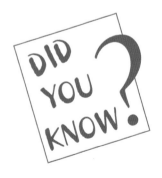

DID YOU KNOW?

Butterflies do not have tongues with taste buds like humans do. Instead, they have taste receptors on the bottoms of their feet. Female butterflies use their feet to taste different plants and lay eggs only on the plant the caterpillars will eat, called a host plant. Female Xami Hairstreak butterflies lay eggs one at a time, moving from leaf to leaf on the host plant.

PLANT PICTURED
Dandelion

Y

1 ⅜ to 1 ¾ inches

Prefers forest openings near moist mountain meadows and streamsides.

OTHER NAMES
Gillette's Checkerspot

PLANT PICTURED
Mountain Arnica

Yellowstone Checkerspot

Euphydryas gillettii
BRUSHFOOT FAMILY

The uppersides of the wings have a dark brown background with a reddish orange band crossing both wings. The forewings have two reddish orange bars. The undersides of the wings have black veins with orange and cream markings.

The Yellowstone Checkerspot is found only in the northern Rocky Mountain region from southern Alberta south through Idaho and western Montana and western Wyoming.

The larva is usually black to dark brown with yellow and white stripes and many yellow spines. It feeds on twinberry, bearberry, snowberry, and other plants.

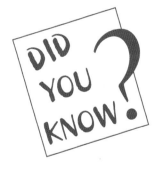

DID YOU KNOW?

The caterpillars feed in groups and live together in silk nests wrapped around several leaves, then overwinter when nearly full grown. At higher elevations, caterpillars may need two winters to become fully developed.

Z

Zerene Fritillary

Speyeria zerene

BRUSHFOOT FAMILY

The uppersides are reddish brown with black markings. The undersides are lighter brown with silvery white markings.

2⅛ to 2¾ inches

The Zerene Fritillary is found from the coast of British Columbia south and east to Montana and south to central California, Arizona, and New Mexico.

Prefers evergreen forest openings, prairies, grasslands, and mountains.

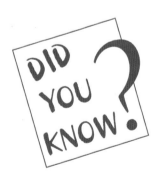

The larva is black with black and yellow spines and two pale stripes on its back. It feeds on violets.

DID YOU KNOW?

Like all butterflies, the Zerene Fritillary has wings covered with tiny scales that overlap like shingles on a roof. These scales give butterflies their color. There are two types of wing colors in butterflies: pigment and structural color. Pigment is the natural coloring within the cells, giving the fritillary the brown and orange colors. To observe structural color, look at the underside of the fritillary's wings. You'll see silvery spots that are caused by light reflecting off the butterfly's scales.

PLANT PICTURED
Purple Coneflower

BUTTERFLY ACTIVITIES

The following activities provide opportunities for children to observe, experiment, and engage in hands-on learning. The projects also encourage children to ask questions, which often leads to further investigation.

CREATIVE WRITING

Picture Poetry

Write a poem using words that describe butterflies. Arrange the words in the shape of a butterfly.

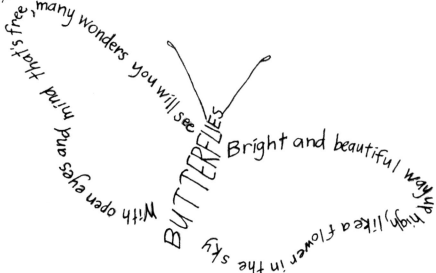

SCIENCE

Gardening

Inviting butterflies to your garden is an excellent way to enjoy them. Butterflies are attracted to brightly colored, sweet-smelling flowers. Some easy-to-grow nectar plants are aster, black-eyed Susan, butterfly bush, butterfly weed, cosmos, bee balm, lantana, marigold, purple coneflower, and zinnia. Check out the website www.kids gardening.org for more information about gardening with kids.

TECHNOLOGY

NABA Butterfly Count

Join citizens all over the United States to identify and count butterflies. Simply register with the North America Butterfly Association on the website www.butterflycounts.org. Scientists use the information to study changes in butterfly populations and to study the effects of weather and habitat change on butterflies. The butterfly count usually occurs each year on the Fourth of July and is similar to the Christmas bird count that Audubon sponsors.

VISUAL ARTS

Butterfly Art

Children of all ages love to create these butterflies that can be hung in the window, on a bulletin board, or just about anywhere. You'll need a white coffee filter, washable markers, a pipe cleaner, and a spray bottle. Flatten out a coffee filter on a paper plate, and color the filter with several different colored markers to make a design. Young children will be more random and that works, too. Spray the coffee filter with water and watch the colors spread and blend. Once it dries, gather the coffee filter in the middle, wrap a pipe cleaner around the center, and curl the ends of the pipe cleaner to make antennae. Fluff the wings, and it's ready to hang!

RESOURCES

CHILDREN'S BOOKS

Boring, Mel. 1996. *Caterpillars, Bugs and Butterflies.* Chanhassen, MN: North Word Press.

Mikula, Rick. 2000. *The Family Butterfly Book.* North Adams, MA: Storey Publishing.

Pfaffman, Garrick. 2009. *Rocky Mountain Bugs.* Basalt, CO: BearBop Press.

GUIDE BOOKS

Brock, Jim, and Kenn Kaufman. 2003. *Kaufman Field Guide to Butterflies of North America*. New York: Houghton Mifflin Company.

Ferris, C.D., and F. M. Brown. 1998. *Butterflies of the Rocky Mountain States*. Norman, OK: University of Oklahoma Press.

Glassberg, Jeffrey. 2001. *Butterflies through Binoculars: The West*. New York: Oxford University Press.

Mikula, Rick. 1997. *Garden Butterflies of North America*. Minocqua, WI: Willow Creek Press.

Neill, William. 2007. *Butterflies of the Pacific Northwest*. Missoula, MT: Mountain Press Publishing Company.

Opler, Paul A., and Amy Bartlett Wright. 1999. *Western Butterflies*. Peterson Field Guide Series. New York: Houghton Mifflin Company.

Poole, Steven. 2009. *Butterflies of Grand Teton and Yellowstone National Park*. Moose, WY: Grand Teton Association.

Pyle, Robert Michael. 1981. *National Audubon Society Field Guide to North American Butterflies*. New York: Alfred A. Knopf.

Stokes, Donald, Lillian Stokes, and Ernest Williams. 1991. *The Butterfly Book*. Toronto: Little, Brown and Company.

Thompson, Bill, III, and Connie Toops. 2011. *Hummingbirds and Butterflies*. New York: Houghton Mifflin.

WEB SITES

http://animaldiversity.ummz.umich.edu. University of Michigan Museum of Zoology's online database of natural history.

http://www.bbc.co.uk/nature. Up-to-date information about Painted Lady butterfly migration.

http://bugguide.net. Identification, images, and information about insects and spiders and their kin.

http://www.butterfliesandmoths.org. Butterflies and moths of North America; includes regional checklists.

http://www.butterfliesofamerica.com. List of American butterflies.

http://butterfly.ucdavis.edu. Art Shapiro's butterfly site; Art Shapiro, professor at University of California–Davis, shares thirty-five years of butterfly population trends in central California.

http://www.kidsbutterfly.org. Includes coloring pages for the Monarch butterfly and galleries of photos.

http://www.naba.org. North America Butterfly Association site; includes information about butterfly gardening and the butterfly count program.

http://www.stopextinction.org. The Endangered Species Coalition provides information about our nation's disappearing wildlife.

http://www.xerces.org. Organization dedicated to preserving invertebrates and their habitat.

GLOSSARY

abdomen. The rear part of an insect's body that contains the organs.

antenna. One of a pair of sensory organs on the head used to touch and smell.

basking. A behavior in which butterflies sit in the sun with their wings open in order to absorb as much of the sun's heat as possible.

chrysalis. The smooth outer covering of a butterfly pupa.

eyespots. Round, eye-like markings on some butterflies and caterpillars. The eyespots look like the eyes of a much larger animal and may scare away predators.

forewings. The two upper wings of a butterfly.

hibernate. To pass the winter in an inactive or resting state.

hindwing. The two lower wings of a butterfly.

honeydew. A sweet liquid that some caterpillars and other insects secrete to attract ants. In turn, the ants help protect them from predators.

host plant. The plant that a caterpillar prefers to eat.

instar. Caterpillar growth period between each molt of old skin.

larva. The caterpillar stage of the life cycle of a butterfly.

life cycle. The four different life stages that butterflies go through: egg, larva, pupa, and adult.

metamorphosis. The process of changing from one form to another during the life cycle of an insect.

migrate. To move regularly from one region to another.

nectar. Sweet liquid produced by many flowers.

overwinter. To live through the winter, often in an inactive state such as hibernation.

proboscis. A tubelike tongue that butterflies use to sip nectar.

puddling. A behavior in which butterflies visit mud puddles to feed on minerals from the soil.

pupa. The stage in a butterfly's life when it is enclosed in a chrysalis. During this stage the caterpillar is changing into a butterfly.

thorax. The front part of an insect's body that contains muscles controlling the wings and legs.

Sharon Lamar's career as an educator has spanned more than three decades, and she has taught students at every grade level from preschool to college. Her two previous children's books, *Montana Moonshadows: A Trek in the Swan Valley Forest* and *Mountain Wildflowers for Young Explorers: An A to Z Guide*, reflect her passionate belief in enriching elementary science education through outdoor investigations, allowing children to connect with nature. As a watercolor artist, Sharon finds inspiration in Montana's towering mountains, dazzling wildflowers, and diverse wildlife. She and her husband, Steve, also an author, make their home in Swan Valley, Montana.